Microsoft Teams

The Microsoft 365 Companion Series

Dr. Patrick Jones

OLYMPUS ACADEMY
PRESS

TABLE OF CONTENTS

MICROSOFT TEAMS: YOUR GATEWAY TO SEAMLESS COLLABORATION

Imagine a workspace where you can chat with your colleagues, host video meetings, share files, and work on documents simultaneously—all without switching between a dozen apps. That's the promise of Microsoft Teams. At its core, Teams is about bringing people together in a unified environment, breaking down barriers, and simplifying how work gets done.

In today's world, where remote and hybrid work are the norm, communication and collaboration tools have become indispensable. Microsoft Teams has emerged as one of the most powerful platforms for connecting teams, facilitating discussions, and ensuring that projects run smoothly. But for many, Teams can feel overwhelming at first glance. Is it a chat app? A meeting tool? A file-sharing platform? The answer is yes—and so much more.

This book is your guide to figuring out Microsoft Teams, whether you're a newcomer just getting started or a seasoned user looking to unlock advanced features. Think of it as a conversation with a knowledgeable friend, walking you through the essentials and sharing practical tips to help you get the most out of Teams.

Throughout these chapters, we'll take a deep dive into Microsoft Teams, exploring its features, capabilities, and best practices. Here's what you can expect:

- **What Is Microsoft Teams?** We'll start with an overview of the platform, breaking down its components and how they fit together to create a seamless experience.

1

- **Why Use Teams?** Discover the unique value Teams brings to your workflows, from improving communication to integrating with other Microsoft 365 tools.

- **Getting Started:** Step-by-step instructions for setting up Teams, creating channels, and customizing the platform to suit your needs.

- **Best Practices:** Tips for organizing your Teams environment, fostering collaboration, and staying productive.

- **Tips and Tricks:** Unlock advanced features like filtering chats, pinning messages, and using keyboard shortcuts.

- **Copilot in Teams:** Learn how Microsoft Copilot uses AI to enhance your Teams experience, from summarizing conversations to automating tasks.

- **Common Pitfalls:** Avoid the mistakes that often trip up new users and keep your Teams environment efficient and effective.

- **Episode Example:** Follow the story of Sarah and her team as they navigate a major project using Microsoft Teams, illustrating the concepts in action.

- **Summary and Reflection:** Recap what you've learned and reflect on how Sarah's journey mirrors your own potential transformation.

- **Final Thoughts:** Tie it all together with encouragement to continue exploring the Microsoft 365 ecosystem.

The workplace is evolving faster than ever, and staying connected is no longer just about convenience—it's essential for success. Teams addresses the challenges of modern work by creating a centralized hub where communication, collaboration, and organization come together effortlessly.

Consider the following scenarios:

- A remote marketing team brainstorming ideas for a new campaign. With Teams, they can chat in real-time, share designs in a channel, and jump into a video meeting for a quick discussion—all in the same app.

- A project manager juggling multiple deadlines and updates. Teams' task integration tools, like Planner, help keep everything organized, while shared channels ensure that stakeholders stay informed.

- An IT department handling technical support. Using Teams, they create dedicated channels for common issues, enabling quick responses and tracking solutions in a structured way.

No matter your industry or role, Teams adapts to your needs, making work more streamlined and effective.

Microsoft Teams is packed with features, which can sometimes feel overwhelming. That's where this book comes in. We'll break down the platform into bite-sized, easily digestible pieces, focusing on practical applications and relatable examples. By the end, you'll feel confident navigating Teams, leveraging its tools, and solving common challenges.

This book isn't just about functionality—it's about transformation. Teams isn't just a communication app; it's a way to rethink how you work, collaborate, and connect. Through relatable stories, like Sarah's journey, you'll see how Teams can solve real-world problems and make a tangible difference in your daily life.

As we begin, it's important to approach Microsoft Teams with curiosity and an open mind. Yes, there may be a learning curve, but the rewards are well worth the effort. Whether you're managing a team, coordinating projects, or simply staying connected with colleagues, Teams has the potential to simplify and enhance your work.

So, let's get started!

WHAT IS MICROSOFT TEAMS?

Microsoft Teams is more than just a communication tool—it's a comprehensive platform that redefines how we connect, collaborate, and organize in the modern workplace. At its core, Teams is a digital hub that brings together chat, meetings, file sharing, and integrated apps into one cohesive space. Designed to work seamlessly with the rest of the Microsoft 365 ecosystem, Teams serves as the central workspace where individuals and teams can communicate and collaborate effortlessly.

Whether you're coordinating a remote team, managing a project, or simply trying to streamline your daily tasks, Teams provides the tools you need to stay productive and connected. But what exactly makes Microsoft Teams so powerful? Let's break it down.

At first glance, Teams might look like just another messaging app, but it's so much more. Its unique combination of features makes it a one-stop solution for work collaboration.

1. **Chat**
   Teams' chat feature allows you to have real-time conversations with individuals or groups. You can send text messages, share files, and even add emojis and GIFs to keep things fun and engaging.

   - o **Example:** Imagine you're working on a report with a colleague. Instead of sending multiple emails, you can quickly share updates, ask questions, and exchange files in a Teams chat.

2. **Channels**
   Channels are like virtual workspaces within a team, designed for focused discussions on specific topics or projects. Each channel can host conversations, files, and even apps related to that topic.

- Example: In a marketing team, you might have separate channels for "Social Media," "Content Creation," and "Campaign Analytics."

3. **Meetings and Calls**
Teams supports audio and video meetings, ranging from one-on-one calls to large webinars. Built-in scheduling tools make it easy to set up meetings, while features like screen sharing, virtual backgrounds, and live captions enhance the experience.

- Example: Sarah, our project manager, uses Teams to host weekly check-ins with her team, sharing her screen to review project timelines.

4. **File Sharing and Collaboration**
Teams integrates deeply with SharePoint and OneDrive, allowing users to store, share, and co-edit files directly within the app. This eliminates the need for constant email attachments and ensures everyone is always working on the latest version.

- Example: Sarah uploads a campaign plan to the "Marketing" channel, and her team members collaborate in real-time to make edits and add suggestions.

5. **Integrated Apps**
One of Teams' standout features is its ability to integrate with a wide range of apps. From Microsoft tools like Planner and Power Automate to third-party apps like Trello and Asana, Teams lets you customize your workspace to fit your needs.

- Example: Sarah adds a Planner tab to her "Project Alpha" channel, giving her team a visual task board to track progress.

Microsoft Teams isn't just a standalone app—it's the centerpiece of the Microsoft 365 ecosystem. By connecting seamlessly with tools like Outlook, SharePoint, and Power BI, Teams acts as a bridge that brings all your work resources together in one place.

- **Outlook Integration:** Schedule and join Teams meetings directly from your Outlook calendar.

- **SharePoint and OneDrive:** Store and collaborate on files shared in Teams using SharePoint and OneDrive.

- **Power BI:** Embed interactive reports and dashboards in Teams channels for data-driven decision-making.

This tight integration eliminates the need to juggle multiple apps, saving you time and creating a more cohesive work experience.

One of the reasons Teams has become so popular is its versatility. No matter your role or industry, Teams adapts to your needs.

- **For Managers:** Teams provides tools for organizing tasks, tracking progress, and keeping everyone on the same page.

- **For Educators:** In education, Teams serves as a virtual classroom, enabling teachers to share lessons, host discussions, and manage assignments.

- **For IT Professionals:** IT teams can use Teams to coordinate projects, monitor system updates, and manage service requests.

- **For Small Businesses:** Even small teams benefit from Teams' collaboration features, which scale seamlessly as the business grows.

While there are many collaboration tools on the market, Microsoft Teams stands out for several reasons:

1. **Seamless Integration with Microsoft 365:** Teams isn't just a tool; it's part of a larger ecosystem that includes apps like Excel, PowerPoint, and Word. This integration allows for a smooth flow of work, with no barriers between tools.

2. **Customization:** From channels and tabs to app integrations, Teams allows you to create a workspace tailored to your specific needs.

3. **Security and Compliance:** Built on Microsoft's trusted cloud infrastructure, Teams includes enterprise-grade security features like data encryption, multi-factor authentication, and advanced compliance tools.

4. **Innovation:** With features like AI-powered Copilot, Teams continues to evolve, staying ahead of the curve and meeting the demands of modern work.

Let's bring this to life with Sarah's journey. When Sarah first started using Teams, she wasn't sure how it would fit into her workflow. But as she explored the platform, she quickly realized its potential.

- **Step 1:** Sarah set up a team for her marketing department, creating channels for different projects like "Content Calendar" and "Social Media Campaigns."

- **Step 2:** She integrated Planner into the "Content Calendar" channel, giving her team a clear visual representation of tasks and deadlines.

- **Step 3:** During team meetings, Sarah used Teams' screen sharing and live captions to ensure everyone was on the same page, even when working remotely.

Within weeks, Teams became the go-to platform for Sarah and her colleagues, streamlining communication and collaboration in ways she hadn't thought possible.

Microsoft Teams isn't just another app—it's a foundation for the modern workplace. By combining communication, collaboration, and productivity into one powerful platform, Teams transforms how work gets done.

Whether you're managing a large project, coordinating with a remote team, or simply looking for a better way to stay organized, Teams has the tools you need to succeed.

WHY USE MICROSOFT TEAMS?

In a world where work happens across time zones, offices, and devices, the way we collaborate has fundamentally changed. Enter Microsoft Teams—a platform designed to keep everyone connected and on the same page, no matter where they are. But why should you use Teams over other tools? What makes it the go-to choice for so many organizations, educators, and individuals?

This chapter dives into the unique value Teams brings to the table, exploring how it enhances communication, fosters collaboration, and integrates seamlessly with the tools you already use. By the end, you'll not only understand why Teams is worth adopting but also see how it can transform your workflow.

1. A Unified Workspace

One of the biggest challenges in modern work is juggling multiple tools to get things done. You might use email for communication, cloud storage for file sharing, and yet another app for meetings. Teams brings all of these elements into a single, cohesive workspace.

- **Example:** Sarah, a project manager, no longer needs to switch between apps to update her team on a project. With Teams, she can send a quick chat, upload a file to the channel, and jump into a video call—all without leaving the platform.

Key Benefit: By centralizing communication and collaboration, Teams reduces context-switching, helping you stay focused and productive.

2. Real-Time Collaboration

Collaboration often involves multiple people working on the same document or project. With Teams, real-time co-authoring and integration with Microsoft 365 apps like Word, Excel, and PowerPoint make it easy to work together without creating multiple versions of the same file.

- **Example:** Sarah's team is preparing a client proposal. Using Teams, they open the Word document directly in the "Proposals" channel and edit it together, seeing each other's changes in real time.

Key Benefit: Teams eliminates the confusion with different versions of a document, ensuring that everyone is always working on the latest version of a document.

3. Seamless Communication

Communication is the backbone of any successful team, and Teams offers multiple ways to stay connected:

- **Chat:** Instant messaging for quick conversations.

- **Calls:** Audio and video calls for face-to-face discussions, no matter where you are.

- **Meetings:** Schedule and host virtual meetings with advanced features like screen sharing, breakout rooms, and live captions.

- **Example:** Sarah uses Teams to schedule her weekly team check-ins. During the meetings, she shares her screen to review progress and uses live captions to ensure nothing is missed, even when connections are unstable.

Key Benefit: Teams adapts to your communication needs, making it easy to stay in touch, whether you're working remotely or in the same office.

4. Integration with Microsoft 365

Teams is built to work seamlessly with the Microsoft 365 ecosystem, enhancing its functionality and making workflows more efficient.

- **Example:** When Sarah creates a new team in Microsoft Teams, a SharePoint site is automatically generated to store shared files. She can also integrate tools like Planner for task management or Power BI for data visualization.

Key Benefit: Teams isn't just a standalone tool—it's a bridge that connects your work across Microsoft 365, creating a unified experience.

5. Customization and Flexibility

Every team is unique, and Teams recognizes that by offering extensive customization options. You can tailor the platform to fit your specific needs, whether through custom tabs, app integrations, or channel organization.

- **Example:** Sarah adds a tab for her team's Planner board in the "Content Creation" channel, giving everyone a clear view of tasks and deadlines without leaving Teams.

Key Benefit: Teams grows with you, adapting to your workflows and helping you stay organized in a way that makes sense for your team.

6. Enhanced Security and Compliance

In an age where data breaches and compliance requirements are top of mind, Teams stands out for its robust security features. Built on Microsoft's trusted cloud infrastructure, Teams includes end-to-end encryption, advanced access controls, and compliance tools.

- **Example:** Sarah's company operates in a regulated industry that requires secure communication. Teams ensures that all chats, calls, and files meet compliance standards, giving Sarah peace of mind.

Key Benefit: Teams combines productivity with peace of mind, ensuring your work remains secure and compliant.

7. Accessibility and Inclusivity

Teams is designed to be accessible to everyone, with features like live captions, transcription, and screen readers. These tools make it easier for people with different needs to collaborate effectively.

- **Example:** During a brainstorming session, Sarah's colleague uses live captions to follow along because they're working in a noisy environment. Another colleague benefits from the meeting transcript to catch up later.

Key Benefit: Teams creates an inclusive workspace where everyone can contribute, regardless of their circumstances.

8. AI and Automation with Copilot

Microsoft Teams isn't just about doing the work—it's about doing it smarter. With the introduction of Copilot, Teams leverages AI to streamline workflows, summarize conversations, and automate repetitive tasks.

- **Example:** Sarah asks Copilot to summarize a lengthy channel discussion, highlighting key decisions and next steps. This saves her time and ensures she doesn't miss important details.

Key Benefit: Copilot turns Teams into more than a tool—it becomes a partner in productivity.

9. Scaling with Your Needs

Whether you're a freelancer working with a few clients or a global corporation managing thousands of employees, Teams scales effortlessly to meet your needs.

- **Example:** Sarah starts using Teams with her small department, but as her company grows, they expand Teams usage company-wide, creating separate teams for HR, IT, and Sales while maintaining centralized governance.

Key Benefit: Teams is as effective for small projects as it is for enterprise-level collaboration.

10. Real-Life Impact: Sarah's Story

Let's revisit Sarah's journey. Before adopting Teams, her team struggled with scattered communication, file chaos, and time-consuming workflows. After switching to Teams, everything changed:

- Team chats replaced endless email chains.
- File collaboration in real-time eliminated version confusion.
- Integrated apps streamlined task management and data visualization.

Sarah's team not only met deadlines more effectively but also found themselves enjoying their work more. The seamless integration of tools and improved communication created a more cohesive, productive environment.

So, why use Microsoft Teams? Because it simplifies the complex, bringing people, tools, and workflows together in one place. It's more than a productivity tool—it's a platform for transformation.

GETTING STARTED WITH MICROSOFT TEAMS: BUILDING YOUR DIGITAL WORKSPACE

Now that you understand what Microsoft Teams is and why it's such a game-changer, it's time to roll up your sleeves and dive in. Getting started with Teams may seem daunting at first, especially with so many features and tools at your fingertips, but don't worry—you don't need to master everything on day one.

This chapter will guide you step-by-step through setting up Teams, customizing your workspace, and laying the foundation for effective collaboration. Whether you're creating a team for the first time or looking to refine an existing setup, this roadmap will help you hit the ground running.

Step 1: Accessing Microsoft Teams

The first step is making sure you can access Teams. As part of the Microsoft 365 suite, Teams is available on multiple platforms, including desktop, web, and mobile.

1. **Desktop App:** Download the Microsoft Teams desktop app for Windows or Mac from the Microsoft website for the best experience.

2. **Web App:** Log in to Teams from your browser via teams.microsoft.com. This is a great option if you're working on a shared or temporary device.

3. **Mobile App:** Download the Teams mobile app from your device's app store to stay connected on the go.

Pro Tip: Use the desktop app for advanced features, but keep the mobile app handy for quick updates and notifications.

Step 2: Setting Up Your First Team

Once you've accessed Teams, it's time to create your first team—a digital workspace for collaboration.

1. **Click "Join or Create a Team"**
   On the Teams dashboard, you'll find the option to create a team. Click it to get started.

2. **Choose a Team Type**
   Teams offers several templates to suit different needs. If not prompted there is an option for More Team Options to select from a variety of templates:

3. **Name Your Team and Add a Description**
   Choose a clear, descriptive name for your team, like "Marketing Department" or "Project Alpha." Adding a short description can help new members understand the team's purpose.

4. **Set Privacy Options**
   Decide whether your team will be private (invite-only) or public (open to everyone in your organization). For sensitive projects, private is usually the way to go.

5. **Add Members**
   Invite team members by typing their names or email addresses. You can also add them later if you're not sure who needs access right away.

Step 3: Creating and Organizing Channels

Channels are where the real work happens in Teams. Think of them as dedicated spaces for specific topics, projects, or discussions within your team.

- **Start with General:** Every team comes with a default "General" channel. Use this for high-level announcements or discussions that apply to the whole team.

- **Add Topic-Specific Channels:** Create additional channels for specific purposes, like "Content Creation," "Budget Planning," or "Client Feedback."

Pro Tip: Use clear, descriptive names for your channels to make navigation intuitive.

Step 4: Customizing Your Workspace

Microsoft Teams allows you to tailor your workspace to fit your team's needs.

1. **Add Tabs to Channels**
   Each channel can have tabs at the top for quick access to files, apps, or tools. For example:

   o   Add a Planner tab to track tasks.

   o   Link a SharePoint library for easy access to shared files.

   o   Include a OneNote notebook for collaborative note-taking.

2. **Set Up Files**
   Upload important documents directly to the Files tab in your channels. Files stored here are accessible to all team members and can be co-edited in real-time.

3. **Pin Important Messages**
   Keep key messages or instructions at the forefront by pinning them to the channel.

Step 5: Inviting External Guests

Teams makes it easy to collaborate with people outside your organization, such as clients or contractors.

- **How to Add Guests:**
  Go to the team settings and select "Add Member." Enter the guest's email address, and Teams will send them an invitation.

- **Guest Permissions:**
  Control what guests can see and do, such as accessing files or posting messages, to maintain security.

Step 6: Scheduling and Hosting Meetings

Teams is well-known for its robust meeting capabilities. Here's how to get started:

1. **Schedule a Meeting**
   In the Teams calendar, click "New Meeting." Fill in the details, including the title, attendees, date, time, and location (online via Teams or hybrid).

2. **Customize Your Meeting Options**
   - Enable waiting rooms for added security.
   - Allow or restrict screen sharing.
   - Record meetings for future reference.

3. **Host Your Meeting**
   During the meeting, use features like screen sharing, live captions, and meeting notes to enhance productivity.

Pro Tip: Use breakout rooms for brainstorming sessions or group discussions.

Step 7: Exploring App Integrations

One of Teams' greatest strengths is its ability to integrate with apps. Start by exploring the Microsoft apps built into Teams, like:

- **Planner:** For task management.
- **Forms:** To collect feedback or run quick polls.
- **Power Automate:** For creating workflows.

As you get comfortable, experiment with third-party apps like Trello and Asana to further enhance your workspace.

Step 8: Getting Your Team Onboard

The success of Teams depends on how well your team adopts it. Help them get started with these tips:

- **Provide Training:** Host a Teams demo or share resources to familiarize your team with the basics.
- **Start Small:** Focus on one or two key features, like chat and file sharing, before introducing more advanced tools.
- **Encourage Engagement:** Use @mentions, emojis, and GIFs to make communication fun and interactive.

Now that you've set up Teams and explored its core features, you're ready to dive deeper into best practices for using it effectively. In the next chapter, we'll share strategies for organizing your Teams environment, fostering collaboration, and staying productive. Let's keep building your Microsoft Teams mastery!

BEST PRACTICES FOR USING MICROSOFT TEAMS EFFECTIVELY

Microsoft Teams is an incredibly powerful tool, but like any platform, its success depends on how you use it. With its range of features for communication, collaboration, and organization, Teams can streamline your workflow and enhance productivity—if you set it up thoughtfully and follow some key best practices.

This chapter explores strategies to help you make the most of Teams, from organizing your workspace to fostering collaboration and maintaining security. By applying these best practices, you'll not only work smarter but also create a more cohesive and efficient environment for your team.

1. Define Clear Purposes for Teams and Channels

One of the first steps to success with Teams is setting clear intentions for each team and channel you create.

- **The Pitfall:** Creating too many teams or channels without a clear purpose can lead to confusion and low engagement.
- **Best Practice:**
    o Define the goal of each team (e.g., "Marketing Team" for departmental projects or "Project Alpha" for a specific initiative).
    o Create channels within teams for focused topics, such as "Social Media Strategy" or "Budget Planning."

Pro Tip: Add channel descriptions to clarify their purpose for new members.

2. Establish Naming Conventions

Consistency in naming teams, channels, and files is crucial for maintaining an organized environment.

- **Example:** Use formats like "Team_Department_ProjectName" for team names and "Topic_Task" for channel names.

- **Why It Matters:** Clear naming conventions make navigation intuitive and help users find what they need quickly.

Pro Tip: Document your naming conventions in a shared "How to Use Teams" channel or file.

3. Keep Communication Organized

Teams offers multiple ways to communicate, from chats to posts in channels. Use these tools effectively to keep conversations relevant and easy to follow.

- **Use Chat for Quick Questions:** Reserve private chats for quick one-on-one or small group discussions.

- **Post in Channels for Team-Wide Updates:** Use channel posts for broader discussions or important announcements.

- **Threaded Conversations:** Reply to specific messages within a thread to keep discussions focused and avoid clutter.

Pro Tip: Use @mentions to draw attention to specific people or groups, like "@MarketingTeam."

4. Leverage Tabs and Apps for Productivity

Teams allows you to add tabs and apps to channels, making it easy to access key tools and information.

- **Example:** Add a Planner tab for task management, a Power BI dashboard for data tracking, or a OneNote notebook for shared notes.

- **Why It Matters:** Tabs centralize resources, reducing the need to switch between apps and improving team efficiency.

Pro Tip: Regularly review tabs to ensure they're relevant and up-to-date.

5. Foster Engagement and Collaboration

Encouraging active participation is key to making Teams a vibrant and productive space.

- **Celebrate Successes:** Use Teams to recognize accomplishments, whether it's completing a project or achieving a milestone.
- **Use Fun Features:** Emojis, GIFs, and stickers can make communication more engaging and foster a sense of community.
- **Collaborate in Real-Time:** Use co-authoring features in Word, Excel, or PowerPoint to work together directly in Teams.

Pro Tip: Host team-building activities in a dedicated channel to strengthen connections and morale.

6. Automate Repetitive Tasks

Teams integrates seamlessly with Power Automate, allowing you to automate tasks and workflows.

- **Example:** Set up a workflow that sends reminders for overdue tasks or automatically archives files older than six months.
- **Why It Matters:** Automation saves time and ensures that nothing falls through the cracks.

Pro Tip: Start with Power Automate templates to simplify the setup process.

7. Maintain a Clean and Organized Workspace

Over time, Teams can become cluttered with unused channels, outdated files, and irrelevant conversations. Regular maintenance is essential.

- **Archive Old Teams:** When a project ends, archive the corresponding team to keep your environment tidy.

- **Delete Irrelevant Channels:** Periodically review channels to ensure they're still active and necessary.

- **Clean Up Files:** Use SharePoint or OneDrive integrations to organize and archive files systematically.

Pro Tip: Schedule quarterly cleanups to keep your Teams environment efficient.

8. Set and Enforce Permissions Carefully

Teams provides granular permission settings, which are invaluable for maintaining security and privacy.

- **Example:** Limit guest access to specific channels or files to ensure sensitive information stays protected.

- **Why It Matters:** Proper permissions prevent accidental data exposure and ensure compliance with organizational policies.

Pro Tip: Use Teams roles, like Owners and Members, to manage access efficiently.

9. Utilize Meeting Features Fully

Teams meetings offer advanced features that can enhance collaboration and productivity.

- **Use Meeting Notes:** Document key points and action items directly within the meeting for easy reference later.

- **Leverage Breakout Rooms:** Divide participants into smaller groups for brainstorming or focused discussions.

- **Record Meetings:** Enable recording for important discussions, ensuring that absent team members can catch up.

Pro Tip: Use live captions to improve accessibility and help participants stay engaged.

10. Encourage Feedback and Continuous Improvement

Teams is a flexible platform that evolves with your needs. Encourage feedback from your team to identify areas for improvement.

- **Example:** Create a "Suggestions" channel where team members can share ideas or report challenges.

- **Why It Matters:** Listening to your team fosters a sense of ownership and ensures that Teams remains a valuable tool for everyone.

Pro Tip: Regularly review usage analytics to understand how your team interacts with Teams and identify opportunities for optimization.

By following these best practices, you'll create a Teams environment that's organized, efficient, and enjoyable to use. These strategies not only streamline workflows but also foster a culture of collaboration and innovation.

TIPS AND TRICKS FOR MASTERING MICROSOFT TEAMS

Microsoft Teams is packed with features, and while the basics are straightforward, there's a treasure trove of hidden tools and shortcuts that can take your experience to the next level. This chapter is all about those "aha!" moments—tips and tricks that will help you work smarter, save time, and get the most out of Teams.

Whether you're a new user or a seasoned pro, these insights will give you fresh ways to navigate the platform, streamline workflows, and make collaboration even easier.

1. Master Advanced Search Features

Finding information in Teams can be daunting if you're navigating manually, but the search bar at the top of the app is a powerful tool.

- **Search for Messages and Files:** Use keywords to locate conversations or documents.

- **Refine Results:** Use filters to narrow your search by team, channel, or time period.

- **Use Commands:** Type /files to see recently shared files or /unread to view unread messages.

Pro Tip: Use quotation marks to search for exact phrases, like "marketing strategy presentation."

2. Pin Important Items for Quick Access

Keep frequently used chats, files, and apps at your fingertips by pinning them.

- **Pin Chats:** Right-click on a chat and select "Pin" to keep it at the top of your chat list.

- **Pin Channels:** Pin essential channels to the sidebar for easy navigation.

- **Pin Files:** Pin a file to a channel's tab or your personal dashboard for quick access.

Pro Tip: Use the "Files" tab in the left navigation pane to view and pin recently accessed files.

3. Use @Mentions Strategically

@Mentions are a great way to grab someone's attention, but overuse can lead to notification fatigue.

- **Mention Individuals:** Use @Name to tag someone for a specific task or question.

- **Mention Groups:** Tag an entire team with @TeamName for announcements.

- **Mention Channels:** Use @ChannelName to notify members about updates in a specific channel.

Pro Tip: Encourage your team to reserve @Team mentions for critical updates to maintain their effectiveness.

4. Customize Your Notifications

Notifications are vital, but too many can be overwhelming. Customize them to focus on what matters most.

- **Set Channel Notifications:** Choose between "All Activity," "Mentions and Replies," or "Off" for each channel.

- **Mute Conversations:** Quiet unnecessary chats by clicking the ellipsis (...) and selecting "Mute."

- **Priority Notifications:** Mark certain chats as priority to ensure you're alerted immediately.

Pro Tip: Adjust notification settings in the mobile app to prevent interruptions during personal time.

5. Leverage Immersive Reader for Accessibility

Teams includes an Immersive Reader feature that makes reading messages easier for everyone, especially those with visual impairments or language barriers.

- **How to Use:** Hover over a message, click the ellipsis (...), and select "Immersive Reader."

- **Features:** Change text size, adjust spacing, or enable text-to-speech for improved readability.

Pro Tip: Use Immersive Reader in multilingual teams to translate messages into different languages.

6. Schedule Messages for the Perfect Timing

Need to send a message but don't want to disturb someone late at night? Schedule it instead.

- **How to Schedule:** In the chat window, click the "Send Later" option (usually represented by a clock icon). Select the date and time for your message to be delivered.

Pro Tip: Use this feature to queue messages for team members in different time zones.

7. Make Use of Breakout Rooms in Meetings

Breakout rooms are perfect for brainstorming or focused group discussions during larger meetings.

- **How to Use:** As a meeting organizer, click the "Breakout Rooms" icon and assign participants to rooms manually or automatically.

- **Switch Between Rooms:** Move between breakout rooms to check in on different groups.

Pro Tip: Use the chat feature in each breakout room to share links or instructions.

8. Integrate Useful Apps and Bots

Teams integrates with a wide array of apps and bots to extend its functionality.

- **Apps:** Add tools like Trello, Asana, or Power BI directly into Teams for task tracking or data visualization.

- **Bots:** Use bots like Polly for quick polls or SurveyMonkey for detailed feedback.

Pro Tip: Explore the Teams App Store to find integrations that fit your team's unique needs.

9. Collaborate on Whiteboards During Meetings

Use the built-in Microsoft Whiteboard app for brainstorming sessions or visual collaboration.

- **How to Use:** During a meeting, click the "Share" icon and select "Whiteboard."

- **Features:** Add text, draw freehand, or use templates for structured brainstorming.

Pro Tip: Save whiteboards to your OneDrive or SharePoint after meetings for future reference.

These tips and tricks will help you unlock the full potential of Microsoft Teams, turning it into a powerhouse for productivity and collaboration. Whether you're customizing your notifications, mastering keyboard shortcuts, or exploring app integrations, each tweak brings you closer to an optimized workflow.

COPILOT IN MICROSOFT TEAMS: YOUR AI-POWERED ASSISTANT

Imagine having a personal assistant embedded in your Microsoft Teams workspace—one that helps summarize lengthy conversations, drafts responses, creates meeting agendas, and even automates workflows. That's exactly what Microsoft Copilot brings to Teams. Powered by AI, Copilot revolutionizes how you interact with Teams, allowing you to focus on meaningful work while leaving repetitive tasks and data analysis to your digital partner.

This chapter dives into the incredible features of Copilot in Teams and how they can transform your productivity. Whether you're managing a project, leading a team, or simply looking to work smarter, Copilot offers solutions that make your daily workflows smoother, faster, and more effective.

Copilot is an AI-driven assistant integrated into the Microsoft 365 ecosystem, designed to enhance your productivity. Within Teams, Copilot acts as a supercharged collaborator, using natural language processing and data analysis to help you stay organized, communicate effectively, and make informed decisions.

Think of Copilot as your silent partner—one that reads between the lines, extracts key insights, and handles mundane tasks so you can focus on what matters most.

1. Conversation Summarization

We've all been part of a long Teams thread that feels overwhelming to keep up with. Copilot simplifies this by summarizing conversations, highlighting decisions, and outlining action items.

- **Example:** Sarah joins a Teams channel discussion halfway through. Instead of scrolling through dozens of messages, she asks Copilot, "Summarize the key points of today's conversation." In seconds, she has a clear overview, complete with decisions made and tasks assigned.

Pro Tip: Use Copilot's summarization feature to document project updates or catch up after a meeting you couldn't attend.

2. Drafting and Editing Messages

Struggling to compose a response? Copilot can help draft professional, concise messages or even edit your drafts for clarity and tone.

- **Example:** Sarah needs to follow up with her team about missed deadlines. She asks Copilot, "Draft a message addressing the missed deadlines and suggesting a revised timeline." Copilot provides a polished message she can send with minor tweaks.

Pro Tip: Use prompts like "Make this message more formal" or "Add a friendly tone to this email" to adjust drafts to your needs.

3. Meeting Preparation and Follow-Up

Meetings often require extensive preparation, from creating agendas to summarizing outcomes. Copilot streamlines this process by handling the details for you.

- **Before Meetings:** Ask Copilot to draft an agenda based on previous discussions in the channel.

- **During Meetings:** Use Copilot to take notes and capture action items automatically.

- **After Meetings:** Have Copilot generate a summary with assigned tasks and decisions, then share it with participants.

- **Example:** Sarah is running a project kickoff meeting. She asks Copilot to "Create an agenda for the kickoff meeting based on the discussion in the 'Project Alpha' channel." The AI pulls relevant points and crafts a structured agenda.

Pro Tip: Use Copilot to send automated follow-up emails summarizing the meeting and including next steps.

4. Insights and Analytics

Copilot can analyze data shared within Teams and provide actionable insights, helping you make informed decisions without switching tools.

- **Example:** Sarah asks, "What were the sales trends from last quarter's reports in this channel?" Copilot generates a clear summary, complete with visuals.

Pro Tip: Combine Copilot with Power BI integrations for more robust data visualizations and insights.

5. Task Management and Automation

Managing tasks across multiple projects can be overwhelming. Copilot integrates with tools like Planner and To Do to streamline task management and even automate workflows using Power Automate.

- **Example:** Sarah assigns tasks to her team during a meeting. Afterward, she asks Copilot to "Add these tasks to Planner and assign them to the respective team members."

Pro Tip: Automate recurring tasks by asking Copilot to set up workflows, like sending weekly reminders for status updates.

6. Real-Time Translation and Accessibility

Collaboration in Teams often spans languages and abilities. Copilot helps bridge these gaps with real-time translation and accessibility tools.

- **Example:** Sarah is working with a global team. She asks Copilot, "Translate this chat into French for the Paris team," ensuring seamless communication.

Pro Tip: Use Copilot to transcribe meetings or enable live captions for better accessibility.

7. AI-Powered Search

Finding specific information in Teams can be a challenge, especially in large organizations. Copilot enhances search functionality with AI-driven capabilities.

- **Example:** Sarah asks, "Find the presentation draft shared last week in the 'Marketing' channel," and Copilot surfaces the exact file instantly.

Pro Tip: Use natural language queries to search for details, like "Show me the last three reports shared by John."

How to Get Started with Copilot in Teams

1. **Enable Copilot:** Ensure your Microsoft 365 subscription includes Copilot, and check with your IT administrator to enable it in Teams.

2. **Start with Simple Prompts:** Use natural language to ask Copilot for assistance, like "Summarize this channel discussion" or "Schedule a meeting with the team."

3. **Experiment with Features:** Explore its capabilities by trying out various prompts and use cases.

4. **Combine with Other Tools:** Integrate Copilot with apps like Planner, Power Automate, and OneNote for a seamless experience.

Pro Tip: Don't hesitate to ask Copilot, "What can you do in Teams?" to explore its full range of features.

Microsoft Copilot in Teams is more than just a tool—it's a game-changer. By simplifying complex tasks, enhancing communication, and automating workflows, Copilot frees you to focus on what truly matters.

COMMON PITFALLS WHEN USING MICROSOFT TEAMS AND HOW TO AVOID THEM

Microsoft Teams is a powerful platform, but even the best tools come with a learning curve. Without a clear strategy, it's easy to fall into common traps that hinder productivity and frustrate users. The good news? Most pitfalls can be avoided with a bit of awareness and proactive planning.

This chapter explores the most frequent mistakes people make with Teams and provides actionable solutions to help you navigate them. By understanding these challenges, you'll be better equipped to maintain an efficient, organized, and collaborative Teams environment.

1. Creating Too Many Teams and Channels

The Pitfall: Overenthusiastic creation of teams and channels can lead to chaos. When there are too many options, users struggle to find the right place for discussions, and important information gets lost.

How to Avoid It:

- **Define a Structure:** Plan your Teams environment before creating anything. Group related channels under a single team instead of creating multiple teams for similar purposes.

- **Limit Creation Permissions:** Restrict who can create new teams to prevent unnecessary duplication.

- **Archive or Delete Inactive Teams:** Regularly review your teams and channels to identify and remove unused ones.

Example: Sarah's organization had 20 teams for overlapping projects. By consolidating them into broader categories like "Marketing" and "Operations," they reduced confusion and improved collaboration.

2. Neglecting Proper Onboarding

The Pitfall: Users unfamiliar with Teams often revert to old habits, like email or shared drives, limiting adoption and creating inefficiencies.

How to Avoid It:

- **Provide Training:** Host introductory sessions or share how-to guides tailored to your organization's use case.

- **Start Simple:** Introduce basic features like chat and file sharing before diving into advanced tools.

- **Assign Champions:** Designate team members as "Teams Champions" to assist with onboarding and answer questions.

Example: Sarah's company struggled with Teams adoption until they held weekly "Teams 101" workshops. These sessions covered key features and encouraged users to experiment.

3. Overloading Notifications

The Pitfall: Excessive notifications can overwhelm users, leading them to mute channels or ignore important updates.

How to Avoid It:

- **Customize Notifications:** Encourage team members to adjust their notification settings to match their preferences.

- **Use @Mentions Wisely:** Avoid tagging entire teams or channels unless it's truly necessary.

- **Summarize Key Updates:** Pin important posts or use channel announcements to highlight critical information.

Example: Sarah's marketing team reduced notification fatigue by creating a weekly "Highlights" post summarizing updates instead of constant individual notifications.

4. Mismanaging File Storage

The Pitfall: Without clear guidelines, file storage in Teams can become a free-for-all, leading to duplicate files, outdated versions, and cluttered libraries.

How to Avoid It:

- **Use Version Control:** Teach your team to edit files directly in Teams to maintain version history.

- **Set File Naming Conventions:** Establish a standard format for file names, like "ProjectName_Date_Version."

- **Leverage Tabs:** Pin important files to the top of a channel for easy access.

Example: Sarah's team created a shared document titled "MarketingPlan_Latest" and agreed to always update it in Teams. This eliminated confusion over which version to use.

5. Ignoring Permissions Management

The Pitfall: Poorly managed permissions can lead to accidental data exposure or unauthorized edits.

How to Avoid It:

- **Use Team Roles:** Assign roles like Owners, Members, and Guests to control access.

- **Limit Guest Permissions:** Review and restrict what external collaborators can see or do.

- **Regularly Audit Permissions:** Periodically check access settings to ensure they align with your current needs.

Example: Sarah's IT department implemented a quarterly permissions review, catching and correcting several outdated guest access settings.

6. Lack of Channel Organization

The Pitfall: Channels without a clear structure can confuse team members and make it difficult to locate information.

How to Avoid It:

- **Group by Purpose:** Create channels based on projects, tasks, or topics.

- **Add Descriptions:** Use channel descriptions to clarify their purpose.

- **Archive Inactive Channels:** Clean up old channels to keep the workspace tidy.

Example: Sarah's team renamed vague channels like "Stuff" to "Client Feedback" and added clear descriptions, improving navigation.

7. Not Utilizing Integrations and Automations

The Pitfall: Failing to integrate Teams with other tools can limit its potential, leaving workflows fragmented.

How to Avoid It:

- **Explore Integrations:** Link Teams with apps like Planner, Power Automate, and OneNote for streamlined workflows.

- **Automate Repetitive Tasks:** Use Power Automate to set up reminders, approvals, or notifications.

- **Encourage Exploration:** Empower team members to experiment with integrations that fit their roles.

Example: Sarah automated task reminders for her team using Power Automate, saving hours of manual follow-ups each week.

8. Overlooking Accessibility Features

The Pitfall: Teams' accessibility features often go unused, limiting inclusivity for team members with specific needs.

How to Avoid It:

- **Enable Live Captions:** Use live captions during meetings for clarity.

- **Explore Immersive Reader:** Offer tools like Immersive Reader to improve readability for all users.

- **Provide Training:** Highlight accessibility features during onboarding sessions.

Example: Sarah's team adopted live captions for all meetings, benefiting non-native speakers and employees in noisy environments.

9. Failing to Monitor Usage and Feedback

The Pitfall: Without monitoring how Teams is used, it's hard to identify pain points or areas for improvement.

How to Avoid It:

- **Review Usage Reports:** Use Teams analytics to track activity levels and engagement.

- **Create a Feedback Loop:** Set up a "Suggestions" channel or periodic surveys to gather input from users.

- **Iterate and Improve:** Act on feedback to optimize the Teams environment.

Example: Sarah's organization added a "Feedback" channel, where users shared ideas like reorganizing channels and pinning frequently asked questions.

10. Treating Teams as a Standalone Tool

The Pitfall: Failing to integrate Teams with the broader Microsoft 365 ecosystem limits its potential.

How to Avoid It:

- **Leverage SharePoint and OneDrive:** Use SharePoint for team file storage and OneDrive for personal files.

- **Integrate with Outlook:** Schedule and manage Teams meetings directly from your Outlook calendar.

- **Combine with Copilot:** Use AI-driven Copilot to automate tasks, summarize discussions, and streamline workflows.

Example: Sarah's team transformed their productivity by using Teams as the central hub, integrating apps like Power BI and Planner to create a seamless workflow.

By addressing these common pitfalls, you can create a Teams environment that's intuitive, efficient, and user-friendly. Remember, the key to success is staying proactive—regularly reviewing your setup, seeking feedback, and adapting to your team's evolving needs.

SARAH'S MICROSOFT TEAMS REVOLUTION

Sarah leaned back in her chair, overwhelmed by the flurry of unread emails, missed calls, and scattered project documents. As a marketing manager leading a team of ten, she had always prided herself on her ability to juggle tasks, but lately, it felt like the chaos was winning. Deadlines loomed, meetings overlapped, and her team seemed perpetually out of sync.

"I need a better way to do this," she muttered, staring at her cluttered desktop. That's when her company rolled out Microsoft Teams.

At first, Sarah was skeptical. She'd heard of Teams but assumed it was just another chat app. The IT department hosted a training session, and while Sarah understood the basics, she wasn't convinced it could solve her team's problems. She reluctantly created a team called "Marketing Department" and invited her colleagues to join.

The initial weeks were bumpy. Messages piled up in the "General" channel, files were uploaded without clear naming conventions, and her team kept defaulting to email for important updates. It felt like Teams was adding to the chaos rather than reducing it.

But Sarah wasn't ready to give up. Determined to make it work, she dug into the platform, exploring features she hadn't noticed before.

One evening, Sarah decided to restructure the "Marketing Department" team. She created channels for specific projects—"Content Calendar," "Social Media Campaigns," and "Client Presentations." In each channel, she added tabs for relevant tools, like a Planner board for tasks and a OneNote notebook for meeting notes. She also set up a SharePoint library to store files, ensuring that everyone had access to the latest versions.

The next morning, Sarah introduced the changes to her team. "We're going to give this structure a shot," she said during their weekly check-in.

"Everything you need for each project will now live in its channel. No more hunting for files or sifting through endless email threads."

Her team was hesitant but agreed to try.

A week later, Sarah saw the first signs of progress. Her team was working on a social media campaign for a new product launch. Instead of bouncing between email and shared drives, they uploaded all assets—graphics, captions, and schedules—to the "Social Media Campaigns" channel. Discussions happened in threaded conversations, keeping the dialogue focused and easy to follow.

During a meeting to finalize the campaign, Sarah shared her screen in Teams and walked everyone through the Planner board. Tasks were assigned, deadlines set, and priorities clarified—all in real time. The meeting ended ten minutes early, a rarity for her team.

"I can't believe how smooth that was," Sarah's graphic designer said as they logged off.

As her team became more comfortable with Teams, Sarah decided to experiment with Microsoft Copilot. She'd heard it could summarize conversations, draft messages, and even automate workflows, but she wasn't sure how it would fit into her workflow.

One afternoon, Sarah asked Copilot to summarize the past week's activity in the "Client Presentations" channel. Within seconds, Copilot generated a concise overview, highlighting decisions made and tasks assigned. Sarah shared the summary with her team, saving everyone time.

Later, when Sarah needed to send a follow-up message to a client, she asked Copilot, "Draft a professional email summarizing today's discussion and requesting feedback on the presentation draft." The result was polished and professional, requiring only minor edits.

"This is a game-changer," Sarah thought.

Just as Sarah felt her team had hit its stride, a crisis struck. A client requested last-minute changes to a major presentation, with only 24 hours until the deadline. In the past, such a situation would have caused panic, with frantic emails and scattered files making things worse.

This time, Sarah turned to Teams. She created a new channel called "Client X Emergency Updates" and added the necessary team members. Using the Files tab, she uploaded the presentation draft, inviting real-time collaboration. Copilot helped summarize the client's feedback and draft an action plan.

Sarah assigned tasks in the Planner tab, and her team worked late into the night, making edits directly in Teams. By morning, the presentation was ready, and the client was impressed with the swift turnaround.

Six months after adopting Teams, Sarah's workflow looked completely different. Her team was more organized, meetings were shorter and more focused, and projects moved forward with fewer hiccups. Teams had become their central hub for communication, collaboration, and task management.

Sarah reflected on the transformation. What had started as a reluctant experiment had evolved into a tool that saved her team countless hours and improved their morale. Even her most skeptical colleagues admitted they couldn't imagine going back to their old ways.

Sarah's story is a testament to the power of Microsoft Teams when used effectively. Her journey wasn't without challenges, but by embracing the platform's features and fostering a culture of collaboration, she turned chaos into clarity.

What could Teams do for you? Whether you're facing scattered communication, disorganized projects, or a team struggling to stay aligned, Teams has the tools to help. Like Sarah, you'll discover that with a bit of effort and a willingness to learn, Teams can transform how you work and connect.

SUMMARY AND REFLECTION: MASTERING MICROSOFT TEAMS

As we near the end of this journey, it's time to step back and reflect on everything you've learned about Microsoft Teams. This powerful platform offers tools to streamline communication, foster collaboration, and bring clarity to your work. It's more than just an app; it's a hub for modern productivity, designed to adapt to your unique needs.

Throughout this book, we've explored Teams from every angle, building a comprehensive understanding of how to use it effectively:

- **Introduction to Teams:** We started by laying the foundation, discussing how Teams fits into the Microsoft 365 ecosystem and why it's become a vital tool for modern work.

- **What Is Teams?** You discovered the core features, from chat and meetings to channels and app integrations, and how they all come together to create a unified workspace.

- **Why Use Teams?** We highlighted the unique benefits Teams brings, such as real-time collaboration, seamless integrations, and advanced security features.

- **Getting Started:** With step-by-step guidance, you learned how to set up Teams, organize channels, and invite collaborators.

- **Best Practices:** Tips on organizing your workspace, setting naming conventions, and fostering collaboration ensured you could build a productive environment.

- **Tips and Tricks:** From advanced search techniques to clever uses of notifications, you gained insights to work smarter, not harder.

- **Copilot in Teams:** AI-driven features like conversation summaries, task automation, and real-time translations showed how Teams is constantly evolving to meet modern demands.

- **Common Pitfalls:** By identifying potential challenges and learning how to avoid them, you equipped yourself to maintain an efficient and effective Teams environment.

- **Episode:** Sarah's story provided a relatable example of how Teams can transform your workflow, offering a practical look at the principles in action.

These chapters have armed you with the knowledge and tools to not only use Teams but to master it, shaping it to meet your needs and elevate your productivity.

Sarah's experience with Teams reflects the path many users take. Like Sarah, you might have started with hesitation, unsure of how Teams could fit into your workflow. Perhaps you've felt overwhelmed by its many features or struggled to get your team on board. But just as Sarah discovered, the key lies in persistence, experimentation, and a willingness to adapt.

Let's revisit some key moments from Sarah's story:

- **The Initial Challenges:** Sarah's early struggles with cluttered channels and inconsistent usage are a common experience. Her decision to reorganize and clarify her team's workspace mirrors the process you might go through as you refine your own Teams environment.

- **Discovering Advanced Features:** From using Planner tabs to integrating SharePoint and leveraging Copilot, Sarah's journey showcases how diving deeper into Teams' capabilities unlocks its true potential.

- **Transforming Collaboration:** Sarah's ability to rally her team around Teams as a central hub demonstrates the importance of fostering a collaborative culture. Her success with real-time editing, organized files, and streamlined communication illustrates what's possible when everyone works together.

- **Handling a Crisis:** The emergency client project showed how Teams can shine under pressure. By creating a dedicated channel, using Copilot, and assigning tasks with Planner, Sarah turned chaos into a coordinated effort.

Now, consider your own journey:

- Where are you in your Teams adoption process?

- What challenges have you faced, and how might the lessons in this book help you overcome them?

- How can you use Sarah's story as inspiration to improve your own workflows and foster better collaboration?

Like Sarah, you have the tools and knowledge to transform the way you work. It's not about perfection from the start—it's about progress, one step at a time.

Microsoft Teams isn't just about working more efficiently; it's about creating a workspace that empowers you and your team to succeed. By integrating tools, automating tasks, and fostering clear communication, Teams can help you tackle challenges and achieve your goals.

EMBRACING THE POWER OF MICROSOFT TEAMS AND BEYOND

As we conclude this journey through Microsoft Teams, it's clear that this platform is more than just a tool—it's a catalyst for change. It transforms the way we communicate, collaborate, and organize, offering a flexible and powerful space to adapt to the challenges of modern work. But Teams is only the beginning. It's a gateway to a larger ecosystem of tools within Microsoft 365, each designed to complement and enhance your productivity.

Your time with Teams has shown you its incredible potential:

- You've learned to organize workspaces, create channels, and integrate apps to streamline workflows.

- You've discovered how to leverage features like chat, meetings, and file sharing to foster better collaboration.

- You've seen the transformative power of AI through Copilot, automating repetitive tasks and providing intelligent insights.

More importantly, you've seen how Teams can adapt to your unique needs, whether you're managing projects, leading teams, or working solo.

Much like Sarah's journey, you've likely encountered challenges along the way, but by applying the strategies and best practices outlined in this book, you now have the tools to overcome them.

While this book focused on Teams, it's important to recognize its place in the larger Microsoft 365 ecosystem. Tools like SharePoint, OneDrive, and Power BI work seamlessly with Teams to create a cohesive digital workspace that supports every aspect of your work.

Consider these possibilities:

- **Teams + SharePoint:** Store and organize shared files in SharePoint while accessing them directly in Teams channels.

- **Teams + OneDrive:** Sync personal files with OneDrive and collaborate on shared documents in Teams.

- **Teams + Power Automate:** Automate workflows across your Teams environment to save time and reduce manual effort.

By integrating these tools, you can create an even more connected and efficient workspace, tailored to your goals.

The world of work is constantly evolving, and so is Microsoft Teams. New features, updates, and integrations are introduced regularly, offering fresh opportunities to optimize your workflows. Staying curious and adaptable is key to keeping up with these changes and continuing to grow.

- **Keep Learning:** Explore new features as they're released and experiment with how they can enhance your work.

- **Share Your Knowledge:** Teach your team what you've learned, fostering a culture of collaboration and innovation.

- **Embrace Change:** As your needs evolve, so can your Teams setup. Don't be afraid to restructure channels, integrate new apps, or try different workflows.

This book is part of the Microsoft 365 Companion Series, a collection designed to help you master the tools that power modern productivity. If you've enjoyed learning about Teams, consider exploring the other books in the series:

- **SharePoint:** Dive into the world of file organization, collaboration, and document management.

- **OneDrive:** Discover the personal file storage tool that integrates seamlessly with Teams and beyond.

- **Copilot:** Explore how AI can enhance productivity across the entire Microsoft 365 suite.

Each book is a step forward in your learning journey, offering practical insights and actionable strategies to help you make the most of Microsoft 365.

Sarah's journey with Teams wasn't just about mastering a platform—it was about transformation. Her experience mirrored the potential we all have to adapt, learn, and grow. Like Sarah, you've taken the first steps toward embracing a new way of working.

Now it's your turn to take what you've learned and apply it in your own unique way. Whether you're organizing your first team, experimenting with Copilot, or exploring advanced features, remember that Teams is a tool to support your success, not define it.

Thank you for letting this book be a part of your journey. Writing it has been a privilege, and I hope it has provided you with valuable insights, practical tools, and the confidence to navigate Microsoft Teams with ease.

Your journey doesn't end here. The skills and strategies you've developed will continue to serve you, not just in Teams but across all areas of your work. So, keep learning, keep experimenting, and keep pushing the boundaries of what's possible.

Here's to your continued growth and success in the Microsoft 365 ecosystem. The future of work is waiting—let's create it together!